The Elephants in the Room
How to cope when you are overwhelmed with clutter

Copyright © Lisa Cole 2017

All rights reserved. This book or parts thereof may not be reproduced in any form, stored in any retrieval system, or transmitted in any form by any means – electronic, mechanical, photocopy, recording, or otherwise – without prior written permission of the author.

For permission requests, email info@less-stuff.co.uk

Cover design by Naked Website Design

Proofreader: Thea Watson

Formatting by fiverr.com/TLMason

Audio version read by Hilary Beaton

ISBN: 9781549637506

Imprint: Independently published

It is good to have stuff, but pointless when you have so much stuff you can't find it!

Table of contents

Introduction 9
    Avoid getting overwhelmed 10
    It is ok to have stuff! 10
    Why do we keep things? 11
    Is minimalism for you? 13
    Find your own balance 14
    Enjoy the process 15
CHAPTER 1 Take it slowly 16
    Rushing decluttering can lead to mistakes and regrets 16
    Getting overwhelmed 17
    Getting over enthusiastic 17
    Repenting decluttered treasures 17
    Feeling resentful 18
CHAPTER 2 Bad times to declutter 19
    When you are angry 20
    When you feel bad about your size/shape 20
    When you are blissfully happy 20
    When it's out of season 21
    Do you need a holiday from it all? 21
CHAPTER 3 Make it easy for yourself 22
    Get a decluttering box and decide where the clutter will go 22
    Should you offer your clutter to your friends and family? 23
    Have realistic expectations 24
    Aim low 25
    Make decluttering a habit 25

Steal time to declutter 26

Set up prompts to remind you to declutter 27

Choose decluttering days 27

Reward yourself often 28

CHAPTER 4 Make a start 29

Get rid of the rubbish first 29

Get rid of broken things 30

Start with the easiest place 32

Prioritise - what is bothering you the most? 32

Do one area at a time 33

Pick out the cream of the crop 33

Leave anything difficult until later 34

Leave anything valuable until later 34

CHAPTER 5 How to get rid of things 35

Easy ways to get rid of things 35

    Freecycle www.freecycle.org 36

    Freegle www.ilovefreegle.org 36

    Gumtree www.gumtree.com 36

    Craigslist www.craigslist.org 36

    Scrap metal collectors 36

    Leave it somewhere with a 'free to good home' note attached 37

    Charity bags 37

    Facebook 37

    Give it to a friend 38

Medium hard ways to get rid of clutter 38

    Recycling www.recyclenow.com 38

    Charity Shops (Op/Thrift Shops) 38

    Amazon 39

  Harder ways to get rid of clutter: more money, possibly more stress 39

    Ebay 39

    Etsy and Folksy 40

    Car Boot Sales/Yard Sales.. 40

    Vintage Fairs 40

CHAPTER 6 Reward yourself for decluttering............................ 41

  You deserve rewards 42

  Free non cluttery rewards.. 42

  Upgrading as a reward and a solution 43

CHAPTER 7 If you get stuck 44

    Step 1. Give into it 45

    Step 2. Do something nice 45

    Step 3. Seek calm places... 45

    Step 4. Be kind to yourself 46

    Step 5. Be kind to someone else................................. 46

    Step 6. Choose one thing to declutter....................... 46

CHAPTER 8 Stop getting more stuff 48

  Avoid adverts 49

  Bargains are not bargains.. 49

  Have regular buy nothing days... 50

  Shop online for the boring things.................................... 50

  Treat yourself with experiences and consumables 50

  Have rules 51

  One in, one out.. 51

CHAPTER 9 Getting help from friends 53

  Clarify expectations 54

Have a time limit 55
Define the area you are decluttering 55
Decide how you want it left at the end 55
Moral support 55
Chapter 10 Five guided days of gentle decluttering 56
Day 1 Declutter the small stuff first 58
DAY 2 Get rid of things you will never finish 60
Clutter control strategy for unfinished items 62
Choose 3 projects each month 62
DAY 3 Declutter a kitchen drawer 63
DAY 4 Stuff that will 'come in handy one day' 65
What are you saving it for? 65
DAY 5 Decluttering shelves in 5 minutes 68
BONUS Control clutter in small containers 70
Grouping 70
Here are some ideas: 70
YOU CAN DO IT! 73
Don't just read about it 73
Checklists 75
Are you ready to declutter? 75
Decluttering Checklist 75
Stop getting more stuff checklist 76
Re-cluttering checklist 78
About the author 79

"This works! Lisa's prompts to guide you through the chaos and overwhelm are humorous, sensitive, respectful and always practical. Giving just five minutes a day using her fun and very clever methods makes the process manageable. Before you know it you are seeing results that last without exhausting yourself. This little gem of a book enables you to distinguish between clutter and treasure. Without much time investment you realise that you are looking at 'stuff' differently and have integrated healthy habits for keeping your 'stuff' relevant." Anya

"Lisa's little and often strategy for decluttering works perfectly for me as my health only allows small bursts of energy but it would be equally good for those with a very full and busy lifestyle." Gaynor

"I love gentle decluttering - It's scary looking at a pile of stuff and not knowing where to start, but Lisa's advice has helped me by starting with small and manageable prompts. This encourages me to do a little each day and by the end of the week, I am amazed by what I've achieved !" Sue

"I used to wildly swap from drowning in clutter to violently purging my belongings to streamline my home (later finding I had flung out something irreplaceable in my mindless scouring).

Gentle decluttering takes out the overwhelm. Easy prompts to inspire you to make the small changes to tackle your chaos while keeping your cool." Jenny

"Lisa's prompts are practical and often link to my own clutter hotspots, the questions she suggests to help decide what can go (and what shouldn't) are always incredibly helpful and sensible and her style is encouraging and non judgy. Lisa's methods help decluttering feel manageable and not overwhelming." Helen

"It's the difference between fearing I'll drown, or fully knowing I can do this, without harming myself." Angela

Introduction

Little changes have a big impact

This book is for anyone who looks around their home and despairs at the amount of stuff in it.

It is decluttering with a difference, aimed at real people who love stuff. There is no encouragement to tip out whole cupboards and it is not at all ruthless.

The Elephants in the Room starts with good concrete decluttering strategies. You will learn how to choose the best time to declutter. You will find out how to make it easy to get rid of thousands of things you do not need. You will know how to declutter without getting stressed out or overwhelmed.

Learn how to declutter in an easy and manageable way with *The Elephants in the Room*. This book will hold your hand and walk you through the process.

Avoid getting overwhelmed

Are you daunted by the idea of decluttering and finding it hard to start? The very idea of tipping out whole boxes of clutter and going through them all at once fills me with dread. This can be so bad I don't get further than turning on Netflix and worrying about it later. This book will introduce you to a way of controlling your clutter. It is easy to do and doesn't need lots of energy and time.

You will learn how to break down the overwhelm into very small and easy tasks. And you will be able to get a system into place that helps you every step of the way.

It is ok to have stuff!

It is great to have things. You should be able to keep them if you like them. Even if they are not at all useful, slightly broken and don't look that nice to other people. If you genuinely like them, then keep them. This book will not encourage you to purge your belongings. I believe that the things we own are important to us, and make up part of who we are.

If you are aiming to lead a simpler, less cluttered life, get rid of the stuff you really don't need first. This will make it easier to decide what you want to keep. This book will help you identify the real clutter. You don't need stuff that is useless, takes up space for no reason and even makes you feel bad about yourself. It is fine to have a home filled with things. Those things should mean something to you and should have happy memories. Stuff we have around us should be liked and/or used often.

There is nothing wrong with having stuff; it helps make us who we are. Academic Russell Belk, who writes about collecting, said that our belongings form part of our 'extended self'. Possessions are very important to us, linking us to our past, our family, our peers and to the world.

Some people say they find minimalism liberating. Having a minimal wardrobe can save lots of time in the morning. People say that they feel better with fewer daily choices, less to clean, less to look after. There is a balance between having so much stuff you can never find anything, to having so little you can live out of a rucksack. If you like the idea of living with very little this book will start you on the way. If you want to live a moderately cluttered life, in a home filled with reminders of happy times, this book will get you there.

Why do we keep things?

Feeling bonded to certain objects that are important to us is not only a human trait. I once met a dog and their owner on the beach; the owner was throwing stones into the ocean for the dog to run in and get. Without fail, the dog got the actual stone thrown, out of millions of other options, time and time again. The stone chosen by the owner was important to the dog in some way, it belonged to the owner therefore it belonged to the dog. My cat has a favourite toy, so loved we call it the 'manky thing'; if she can't find it she will howl.

From a very early age we bond with our possessions believing they have what Christian Jarrett calls a 'unique essence'. Even very young children would rather have the toy they had been given minutes earlier than an exact replica. It does not take long for our possessions to become part of us, almost a physical extension of ourselves.

Our belongings connect us with the past. I know many people who love a particular kitchen utensil that came from their grandmother. We keep photos of relatives who died long before we were born because they connect us to our own histories. We lug around antiques of varying value purely because they once belonged to Uncle so and so. Often we cling onto things that mean nothing to us other than a historical connection. We hold onto stuff that reminds us of the past and how we felt. I am never going to get rid of 'Fluff'. This 50 year old bit of rabbit skin was once sewn into a rough kitten shape. Now mended to within an inch of its life, with the big clumsy stitches of a child, it has had one too many brushes with an accidental boil wash. Fluff went everywhere with me when I was little. Still to this day he makes me feel safe and secure, even though he is now tucked away in a cupboard lest the cats mistake him for a manky thing.

Our belongings show others who we are in the world, even if we don't want them to know. From fast red showy sports cars to the muted tones of an environmentally friendly ethical organic t-shirt, the things we choose to have make a statement about who we are.

There is a language of clothes that is delicately nuanced and speaks reams about us before we open our mouths to strangers. We read each other's shoes and bags, we make snap decisions based on what people carry with them. We don't see many bowler hatted men in town centres now but we can easily identify people who might be office managers from their clothes. Any opportunity we have to choose our stuff gives us a chance to display who we are to the world. Even our choices in the supermarket tell other shoppers a lot about us and our habits. There is no escape from this unless you live off-grid and see no other humans.

We need tools that help us get on with life more. We keep things because they connect us with other humans. Belongings help us define our identity and can make us very happy.

Is minimalism for you?

Paring down your stuff to the bare minimum is increasingly fashionable. Bloggers travel the world living out of carry-on bags. Smart and fashionable people write about how freeing it is to have a limited wardrobe. Key influencers of our society wear a self imposed uniform. They share photos of their replicated outfits and we aspire to be like them.

While the idea of extreme minimalism can be attractive, what is the reality?

Pros

- Less cleaning
- Less storage needed

- Easier to find things
- Time saved not choosing what to wear
- Money saved from not shopping

Cons

- You need lots of discipline
- Less choice in every aspect of day to day life
- Need to buy or borrow if you don't have something
- Not prepared for emergencies like power cuts
- You may feel deprived

Find your own balance

There is no need to pare your belongings down to a few items to enjoy some of the benefits of minimalism. Equally, there is no need to live in a home that is so filled with things you cannot move easily in it. Do you have to buy the occasional thing all over again because you can't find the one you have? You can get your stuff down to a manageable level without hiring a skip. You do not need to reduce your belongings down to a backpack. The aim of this book is to help you keep the things that are important to you and that make you feel happy

Enjoy the process

Decluttering doesn't need to be stressful or horrible. It can be easy, painless and even fun. Make a game of it and reward yourself frequently.

Decluttering just a few things a day is a good safe way to make sure that you keep things that are important to you. No one, including your inner voice, should tell you to get rid of things you love. Go gently, tread lightly and allow yourself the time you need to do this.

"I put on music... Having rummaged out my old cassettes I find my energy for decluttering whilst listening to them." Martha

CHAPTER 1
Take it slowly

Slow and steady wins the race

Rushing decluttering can lead to mistakes and regrets

Like a crash diet for belongings, big decluttering purges get rid of stuff in the moment. They can make you overwhelmed and exhausted and they generally don't stick.

It sounds great in theory. Pull all your clothes out of every cupboard and drawer, lay them on the bed (spilling onto the floor if needs be).

Then start to go through them one by one, making boxes or piles for 'keep', 'bin' and 'donate'. In reality there are risks involved in this method and you might find yourself sleeping on the sofa!

Getting overwhelmed

When faced with a huge pile of things to sort through I have a tendency to shut the door on it and run away. It's all too much, seeing it in a huge pile paralyses me and even though I know how to start (start!) I can't do it. I get stuck.

Avoid overwhelm by only decluttering a few things at a time.

Getting over enthusiastic

Going through a huge pile of junk once, I started to chuck out handfuls of paperwork. Including my birth certificate by accident. It's a pain having to get a replacement when you need one.

Avoid throwing out things you need by taking it slowly.

Repenting decluttered treasures

When I am faced with a large number of bin bags for the charity shop I will avoid taking them. This can go on for so long that I forget what is in them. Then I'm at risk of going through them again in case I've changed my mind.

Know where to get rid of your clutter before you are ready to take it there.

Feeling resentful

When I'm going through my things and working out if I 'should' keep them or not I start to feel resentful on many levels. Why shouldn't I keep it? Why can't I live a minimalistic lifestyle like they do on the internet?

Start by decluttering the things that are clearly useless to you first. It's ok to keep things you like.

CHAPTER 2
Bad times to declutter

Choose your best time to declutter

Decluttering doesn't have to be a huge job that requires you to drop everything and take a week off. Avoid the logistics of skip hire and going through the whole house at once. Declutter gently. Slowly. Forget the idea of purging all your stuff and declutter in small doses. You will find that you can fit in a quick 5 minute declutter to daily life very easily. There are however, some times when it is better to wait before decluttering.

It might seem weird reading about when NOT to declutter in a book all about it. We should keep the things we love and some situations provoke us into making bad decisions. Here are some of those situations with solutions.

When you are angry

This is a pretty easy emotion to identify. If you find yourself decluttering in a rage, there is a good chance that you will make some decisions you may regret later. If you need to throw out all his guitars or whatever, go for a good angry walk instead. Leave your money at home so you can't buy something else.

Take some time to breathe and work out what you want.

When you feel bad about your size/shape

I'm not suggesting that you keep all the size 8 clothes you had as a teenager. I know that there is a danger of hating every item of clothing when you hate the shape your body is in. There is nothing you can do about losing/gaining a couple of stone or becoming fitter right this minute. Wait to declutter until you feel less wretched.

Leave decluttering for another day and be kind to yourself.

When you are blissfully happy

'But I'm in LOVE, I don't need shoes because I'm floating with joy!' I hope this feeling lasts a long time and your landing is gentle.

Enjoy the feeling and wait until your feet are on the ground before making decluttering decisions.

When it's out of season

Can you remember how cold it gets in the winter when it is midsummer? In my home we double up on duvets during the winter. This means the airing cupboard is ram-packed during the summer. It would be easy to look in the cupboard and see far too many things out of season. Avoid getting rid of sun hats on a gloomy winter's day. Remember what it is like to squint in the sunshine later in the year.

Declutter seasonal things in season, so you don't get rid of something you need later.

Do you need a holiday from it all?

It is ok to feel like it is all too much, and it is fine to take a break from it.

- If you can, close the door on a particularly cluttered room. Throw a blanket over a nasty looking bookshelf and have a break for a few days.
- Do something very different to recharge your mind. Take a walk, go to the cinema - be aware of the risk of re-cluttering if you are near shops.
- Set a time limit so you don't ignore it forever.
- Remember you don't need to do it all at once.

CHAPTER 3
Make it easy for yourself

Get prepared to make it easier

Get a decluttering box and decide where the clutter will go

Be prepared to get rid of your stuff by having a box for the charity shop stuff on the go. Put the box somewhere you cannot miss it so it reminds you to declutter a little bit every day.

Identify a charity shop to take the box to when it is full; arrange transport or collection if needed. A lot of charity shops will send donations to different areas if you ask them. This way you don't need to risk seeing your old stuff again.

Get the recycling and rubbish out of your house as soon as you can so you have more space.

"Something I started because of the less-stuff Facebook group is having a decluttering box. I used it as a place to put things that could go to the charity shop. I try and put at least 1 thing a day in there (preferably more) and then donate the stuff on Saturday."

Liane

Should you offer your clutter to your friends and family?

Although it is nice to offer stuff you don't want to friends and family this might not be helpful. They may feel obliged to take something, or you might be helping them to add to their own clutter. It might be difficult to see something you decluttered being used in someone else's home. Ask your friends if they are looking out for anything, so you can give them the option of anything suitable you might find.

The exception to this is when you are decluttering objects that have memories for other people. It is unlikely your grown up children will want all the artwork from their primary school years but it is nice to ask in case.

Have realistic expectations

You are human. You cannot do everything at once. When you are faced with an enormous task it can be hard to know where to start. Break decluttering down into tiny chunks and have very small goals to make it work for you. It may feel frustrating at first but doing something, even if it is a tiny thing, is better than doing nothing. Those tiny chunks of decluttering will all add up and you will see results sooner rather than later.

Last year I had a ceiling taken out in my son's bedroom. It was falling down anyway and needed replacing. Weeks after the work ended the whole house was coated in 150 year old dust. Victorian smog that was trapped between the roof and the ceiling had been set free.

I was looking forward to getting some order back into life. My bedroom had all my son's things in it. I'd been living in the same two sets of clothes for a fortnight and I was totally fed up with it. A friend was going to help on the day after the work finished. I imagined my house looking all clean and gorgeous with a day spent on it. My friend had the flu and cancelled. This was a good thing because in reality, there was no way that two people could do what I fantasised over in a day. It was a big job that eventually took weeks with more than one friend helping (the dust kept settling). The friend that cancelled gave me a chance to step back from the huge job. I had time to work out what could be done instead of trying to do it all at once.

If you are faced with a huge task there are a few things you can do to make it manageable. Get rid of the rubbish first, ditch the broken things. Start where a little effort will make a difference or prioritise and work on what is bothering you most. It is worth trying different strategies because this is not a one size fits all solution. You might find that a certain approach is better for different times and different types of clutter. The most important thing is to be prepared and ready to declutter, and just tackle one area at a time.

Aim low

Aim to get rid of 5 things a day, just 5. If the thought of 5 things is too much for you then only get rid of one thing a day. Any movement towards decluttering is better than ignoring it. If you get rid of 25 things a week that is over a thousand in a year. Every little counts.

If you feel like it is all impossible and you will never manage to declutter then try these simple ideas:

- Put one thing away.
- Identify one bit of total junk and throw it away or put it in the recycling.

If you decluttered one thing a day, that would be hundreds over the year. So don't be afraid of starting very small and moving very slowly when it comes to decluttering.

Make decluttering a habit

There is lots of research that says habits can only be established if you do them for a certain number of days. Some say 30 days, some say 5 weeks, some say a habit won't stick unless you do it daily for half a year. Some of these theories might be correct, but I know for myself that sticking to anything for more than 5 days is hard work.

I do have some long term behaviour patterns though. Every morning I wake up. I try not to fall over the cats who are waiting outside my bedroom door. I go to the loo, brush my teeth, go into the kitchen, feed the cats and boil the kettle for a cup of tea. This routine varies ever so slightly on a day to day basis. It depends on how urgently the cats think they need feeding. Generally though, I start my morning without thinking about it that much. I use the toilet, brush my teeth, feed the cats and make a drink. Many things have to be done around the house on a regular basis to keep mess under control. The recycling and bin has to go outside on the right day. Dirty clothes have to be collected, sorted, washed and hung on the line to dry. Although I don't consciously think of these things as habits, they do happen regularly. They generally follow the same pattern. If you can hook a decluttering habit onto an existing one it will get established quickly. Pretty soon you won't have to remember to do it.

Steal time to declutter

What habits or patterns have you already established around your home? Which of them involve an element of waiting? You can use that time for a quick 5 minute declutter.

You might have time while:

- The bath runs
- The washing machine spins
- The kettle boils

- The computer starts up
- You are on a phone call that is on hold

Away from home, you can declutter pockets and bags. You can delete messages and photos from your phone while waiting in a queue.

Set up prompts to remind you to declutter
Is there a drawer in your kitchen that needs sorting out? Leave it open overnight. In the morning it will remind you to pick out a couple of bits of clutter while the kettle is boiling. You might need to put your decluttering box somewhere you have an existing habit to act as a trigger. If you are using the time taken to run a bath, putting your decluttering box in the bathroom will help you remember to put something in it. If it helps you to have a decluttering box in every room then have one, put it somewhere you cannot miss it as a reminder. My decluttering box is in the hallway at the foot of the stairs in a really annoying place. You have to walk around it to get anywhere in the house; I will not forget to add clutter to it because I trip over it daily. It is possible to get used to things that are in the way, so think about changing the location of your decluttering boxes often.

Choose decluttering days
Realistically, you do not want to be decluttering every day for the rest of your life. Aim for weekdays only and increase your chances of success. Decluttering becomes a minor task when you take the pressure off yourself. Forget pulling everything out all at once. Nibbling away at it makes it much easier to control.

Reward yourself often

If you declutter while the kettle is on, your reward could be a cup of tea. You could tell yourself that you can drink the tea when you have got rid of something in the kitchen. The reward doesn't have to happen instantly. You could reward yourself by doing something nice for half an hour after you get the box of clutter out of your home. Get a nice coffee, spend half an hour in the park listening to the birds. Give yourself something to look forward to, it is important to be kind to yourself.

CHAPTER 4
Make a start

Get rid of the rubbish first

Clutter is often composed of total junk you clearly do not need. Magazines that are years out of date but not so old as to be interesting. Packaging from long gone appliances. Single socks or gloves, pens that don't work and out of date medicine are all things that take up space in your home. Spend the occasional 5 minutes skimming off the dregs from your clutter collection. Once the surface layer of rubbish has gone you will be able to see the more important stuff in a clearer light.

"Gradually, as the junk is peeled away, the buried lovely stuff emerges and has space to shine." Jane

Get rid of broken things

Sometimes we can have the very best of intentions but we never get round to mending things. Ask yourself these questions:

- Is it expensive to fix?
- Is it a hassle to mend?
- Will I use it if it is mended?
- Do I have the materials to fix it?
- Do I actually like it?
- Am I just keeping it because someone gave it to me?
- Am I keeping it in the hope it will have value one day?
- Is it a part of something else I lost a long time ago?
- Would something else I have do the same job as it?
- Have I got more than one of them?
- Do I need that many?
- Is it cheap and easy to replace?

If something makes you feel bad, that counts as rubbish too, you don't need to keep things around you that make you feel bad in any way.

THE ELEPHANTS IN THE ROOM

We are not looking for things that stir up huge emotions here, just little things that nag away at us.

Ask yourself these questions:

- Does it remind me of a bad time?
- Does it make me feel sad?
- Does it make me feel guilty?
- Does it make me feel I should do something I probably will never get round to doing?

You can do this in any room and likely candidates are:

- Books you mean to read one day
- Shoes you wore once to an interview you didn't get the job for
- A dress that makes you feel ugly
- A half-knitted cardi for a friends baby who is now in primary school
- Bottles of smelly stuff that you don't like but were given to you so you think you will be ungrateful getting rid of them (you won't!)
- The fish tank for the fish that died and you are keeping it in case you get new ones, one day.

"I still intend to get round to doing my paperwork but I smiled at Lisa's not throwing the baby out with the bathwater method that really is the best! By skimming all the obvious first it's so much easier to not discard something you might need later." Anna

Start with the easiest place

If you are overwhelmed at the start, and you try to tackle the most cluttered area in your home first, you can set yourself up to fail. To get over this, start somewhere where a little bit of work will make a big difference. Where is the least cluttered area in your home? It could be a bathroom cabinet, a shelf, the hallway, anywhere at all. It might help to look around your home and pretend that visitors are about to arrive. Which area looks best? Start decluttering there to see morale boosting results more quickly.

Prioritise - what is bothering you the most?

I get very stressed when I can't find things I need so it is important for me to have paperwork in some sort of order. I also like to be able to find underwear that fits when I need it instead of sifting through a drawer of all sorts. Identify one type of clutter that is really annoying you and deal with that.

Clutter types you might want to prioritise could be:

- Paperwork
- Underwear and socks
- Workwear
- Books
- Music or films

Do one area at a time

If you need inspiration look around your home and pick a spot that is bothering you. One shelf, one box, one corner … choose one area to work on for a few minutes. Or pick something from this list:

- The top of the fridge
- A cupboard
- Under the stairs
- Under the bed
- A drawer
- Underwear
- Plants
- Books
- Food
- Cosmetics
- Towels
- Winter/summer clothes
- Sports equipment
- Gardening tools
- Pictures and ornaments
- Under the sink

Pick out the cream of the crop

Craft projects are often a great excuse to store materials up in advance. If you have been collecting materials for a while there is a good chance you have more than you need. If you have these hoards of things waiting to be used, try allocating a box for the actual amount you need. Put the nicest of your collection into the box and get rid of the rest.

Leave anything difficult until later

Deal with the non-emotive clutter first. This can make a big difference to how you feel about the things you are attached to but are not doing you any good. Get rid of the worthless, broken, useless stuff first because this will be the easiest to say goodbye to. Make space by skimming off the surface rubbish so it will be easier to work out how you feel about the rest of your stuff.

"I found I had to create a box marked "Toxic" to put that sort of stuff in. I shoved loads in without going through it. Then once in a while, when feeling strong I'd just grab the top 5 out and go through them. Most ended up in the bin. I've only got a big brown envelope marked "Toxic" now, mostly with really scarily sad stuff in." Linda

Leave anything valuable until later

If you come across things that are worth a lot of money wait until you have got rid of the worthless stuff first. Do you have something expensive that makes you feel terrible about yourself? It might be better for you to take the hit and donate it but in general, be cautious if you think something is worth a lot. Once the rest of the clutter is down to a more manageable level it will be easier for you to find the energy to sell things.

CHAPTER 5
How to get rid of things

Find a new home for your old things

Having stuff hanging around your house for weeks after you have decided to get rid of it can get you down. There are many ways to get rid of stuff, some easier than others. Let's start with the easiest way.

Easy ways to get rid of things

In an ideal world your clutter would be collected and taken away from you at a time that suited you. This is actually possible and here are some ways to get rid of your stuff that need minimal effort from you.

Freecycle www.freecycle.org

A worldwide network of people who give things away to people who collect them. Great for getting rid of big things (like pianos!) and for decluttering boxes of random stuff for other people to take to a car boot sale. You need to find your local Freecycle group and join it, then you just post what you want to get rid of.

Freegle www.ilovefreegle.org

UK group Freegle say 'Don't throw it, give it away!'. There are 1,462,341 Freegle members in 383 reuse groups all over the UK at the time of writing. It works the same way as Freecycle but in some areas it is more active, which is important when you are getting rid of stuff.

Gumtree www.gumtree.com

Massive UK classified ads site split into areas. It has a free to collector section and it is free to list items.

Craigslist www.craigslist.org

Based in America but covering the world, Craigslist is a classifieds site where you can list things for free and ask people to collect them.

Scrap metal collectors

If you Google 'scrap metal collector in (wherever you are)' there will be a whole bunch of people who will collect your stuff for nothing, then make money on it by weighing it in.

If you prefer to keep the money yourself, but have the hassle of taking it to be weighed in Google 'sell scrap metal' and your location. More recently you have to take ID to the scrap metal merchant to prove the metal is yours to sell.

Leave it somewhere with a 'free to good home' note attached

This works for me nearly every time. I just leave things on the wall at the front of my garden. If they are still there at the end of the day I'll take them to the charity shop instead. They generally go pretty quickly. Just bring them in if it rains.

Charity bags

In the UK charity bags are posted through doors for people to fill up. This is easy as you just leave the full bag outside your house but be aware that the majority of the money made by selling these clothes will not go to a charity. The clothes you donate are sorted into sellable and recycling and then sold to other companies to make money out of. The collectors pay so much to the partner charity per ton collected.

www.charitybags.org.uk says 'Taking your unwanted clothes etc to a charity shop raises around 50 times more money for charity compared with giving your clothes to a typical house-to-house "charity" collector!'

Facebook

There are many local groups for buying, selling and giving stuff away on Facebook. Try searching for 'Buy and Sell' or 'Facebay' in your area. My local group is called BS5 Booty!

Give it to a friend

This only works with things you can bear to see again.

"Giving to someone else really helps. Diminishes guilt. Better things are used by others than languishing in my place. Also, if you are reluctant to part with that really useful item you haven't used for years, there's a chance you could "borrow" it back if you do ever do need it." Patricia

Medium hard ways to get rid of clutter

Recycling www.recyclenow.com
For UK people the Recycle Now website has a handy way of finding out what you can recycle in your recycling box and what your local tip will take. Outside the UK look on your local government website for details of what and where you can recycle.

Charity Shops (Op/Thrift Shops)
This involves you taking the stuff to the shop, though if you have a local one it might be worth asking if they can collect. You might want to avoid some of these if you are not happy about testing on animals – there is a list of charities that do use animal testing here: www.peta.org.uk

Also, some of the bigger charity shops have a reputation for spending more money on shops and management than on the charity. Oxfam is famous for this and the RSPCA are said to destroy half the animals they rescue. Jean Eaglesham wrote an article about the big business of charity shops in the Independent[1] She said 'On average, 73p of every 1 pound you spend is soaked up in the expenses of running the shops'. Personally I try to give my stuff to smaller local animal shelter charity shops or to places like Emmaus who help, home and retrain homeless people. My local one takes clothes and books as well as furniture.

Amazon

You can sell your old books on Amazon for free, the listings stay up as long as you like but you do pay a commission when they sell. This is pretty painless because all you have to do is type in the bar code but then it's a hassle packaging and posting them out. The best thing I think is to check the prices of your books on Amazon first then just sell the ones that are going for the most; ones that sell for 50p you might as well just give away. The only problem with this is that you will have a box of books waiting to be sold and this could take some time.

Harder ways to get rid of clutter: more money, possibly more stress

Ebay

Easier now that you can list items by using the app on a smartphone but this is still a lot of time for (in my experience) very little return

---

[1] https://www.independent.co.uk/money/money-charity-shops-and-the-cash-that-wont-reach-the-needy-1276435.html

and then the worry of getting bad feedback. Watch out for free listing weekends though.

Etsy and Folksy

Etsy has a more American audience than Folksy. On Etsy you can sell vintage clothes, fabric and furniture, on Folksy just fabric unless they have changed the rules recently. It's 20c per item to list on Etsy, 16p to list on Folksy (prices subject to change so please check them). The item stays up for a few months and great pictures are really essential here.

Car Boot Sales/Yard Sales

If you can really stand the thought of a thousand people pawing their way through your stuff and judging it, car boot sales are perfect for you. Personally I'd rather eat my own flesh. One good idea I heard was of friends selling each others stuff, though of course there is a very real danger of buying more stuff than you came in with.

Vintage Fairs

Really popular at the moment, stalls range from £10 to hundreds and kitchenalia seems to sell better than clothes. If you have anything in good condition that is over 30 years old a vintage fair could be a great way to get rid of it and earn some money.

CHAPTER 6
Reward yourself for decluttering

Plan to reward yourself

As you start to declutter gently you will find some things to recycle, some that need to be thrown away and some that can go to a charity shop. It is a good idea to get these out of your house as soon as possible. If you have already decided where the box should go it is just a matter of getting it there. Do you need to arrange transport? Can they collect it for you? Is there a charity shop you could walk it to if it is not too heavy?

You deserve rewards

Old fashioned star charts work well for adults too. It can be a physical or an imaginary chart, just make sure you have a reward at the end of it. The reward doesn't need to involve spending money. You don't need to treat yourself by eating or re-cluttering. A long soak in a bath after you have decluttered your towels is a great reward. Have some time on the sofa under blankets with a good book. Take a nap, go for a long walk, a trip to a museum or library. If you are stuck for ideas here is a list:

Free non cluttery rewards

- Take time for yourself to do nothing
- Phone or Skype a friend
- Take a flask of coffee out and meet someone
- Have a long bath
- Read a book
- Take a nap
- Watch a film
- Listen to music
- Go to a free museum or art gallery (avoid the gift shop!)
- Find some wildlife to watch
- Take your imagination on a cloud journey and build castles with it
- Learn something new and random: YouTube is good for instructional videos
- Take time to doodle for no reason
- Use up something you have been saving for a special occasion
- Wear something you feel great in

Upgrading as a reward and a solution

If you are craving the buzz a new thing can bring, try upgrading to replace something instead of shopping. This is a form of bargaining you can do with yourself sometimes but it won't work on every occasion. It is best to upgrade only if you have something you use often. Find an object that does not work well for you: a jug that pours badly, shoes that pinch, a bag that comes undone. Upgrade something you have been making do with for a while. If your upgrade replaces two things that is all the better. You do not need to spend lots of money to upgrade. A tin opener with a bottle opener on one end could replace two separate tools for a couple of quid. Searching for second hand options can be lots of fun but don't get distracted and buy more clutter!

CHAPTER 7
If you get stuck

Feeling stuck is normal

We all get stuck at some point. It's ok to get stuck. I'm talking about feeling that you cannot make a start and it is all too much too deal with. When I'm stuck I feel slightly panicky and almost paralysed by anxiety. Remember that clutter is emotional stuff as well as physical. Even thinking about it might be exhausting. Gentle decluttering is less likely to bring on total overwhelm. It can still happen and it's good to accept being stuck as totally normal. Be kind to yourself, it will pass. Take a break when you need to, call a friend if that helps. I get stuck a few times a year and I always, without fail, forget what helps me get over it so I have written a list to refer to.

Here are the steps that help me get over a period of stuckness:

Step 1. Give into it

Allow yourself time to sit and wallow in how you feel. It is ok to be overwhelmed, it is ok to find it difficult. Take a deep breath and know that you are not alone and this is perfectly normal. This will help you realise that the stuck feeling is in your head and that it is a reaction to your environment. You can give yourself a time limit if that helps, or you can just see how it goes.

Step 2. Do something nice

If you feel very low on energy, wrap up in blankets and watch a film. Don't beat yourself up about taking this time off. You need to look after yourself so you will be able to face the clutter when you are ready. If you feel a bit more lively you could go for a walk or meet a friend for coffee.

Step 3. Seek calm places

Too much visual stimulation can be stressful and make your senses work too hard. If the overstimulation is coming from clutter you feel pressure to sort out, that will not help you feel unstuck. Find somewhere calm and tidy to be. A quiet spot in a museum or library is good. Outdoors with a big open sky is better. Failing all of that find some calm images on the internet or in a book. The idea is to rest your senses and recharge your energy levels.

"Sometimes I get on my bicycle and go for a ride and come back with renewed vigour. And I always start with getting rid of the rubbish. Sometimes you have to have a clean up in between and this helps you feel better when the house is looking nicer". Martha

Step 4. Be kind to yourself
Realise that in taking time to regroup you are making yourself strong enough to deal with it. Stopping is a positive move sometimes. Squash any nagging voices you might have in your head that tell you that you are failing. You are merely in preparation mode and that is fine. Do something you like doing instead.

Step 5. Be kind to someone else
If you feel vile but have the ability to make someone else's life better it can change things around for you too. Give a book to a homeless person, donate the money you would spend on a coffee to a cause you like or take out a Kiva loan[2] to help someone else by investing in their business. Altruism has been associated with many health benefits and research suggests that helping others can increase your lifespan[3].

Step 6. Choose one thing to declutter
Just one thing, that is all. Find one broken old manky thing you cannot stand the sight of and get rid of it. If getting a box organised for donating is too much for you right now, find something you can recycle or throw away.

---

[2] www.kiva.org

[3] www.mentalhealth.org.uk/a-to-z/a/altruism

If working through these steps to become unstuck does not work for you check with a doctor that you are not depressed. Clutter and depression are sometimes linked in a vicious cycle. Speaking to a professional about how you feel can make a big difference.[4]

---

[4] https://www.webpsychology.com/news/2016/01/11/link-between-clutter-and-depression-251731

CHAPTER 8
Stop getting more stuff

There is little point in decluttering anything unless you are bringing less back into the house than you are taking out. To get a realistic idea of how much stuff you acquire in a week start a list, don't count consumables such as food and drink but list everything else. How much space does it all take up? How much of it is actually useful and will be an invaluable asset to your life?

Here are some good strategies to help you stop filling your house with clutter.

Avoid adverts

It's far too easy to use shopping as a way to relax and get away from it all. It doesn't help that we are bombarded with adverts telling us we need more stuff. Adverts make me feel like a failure. My hair will never be glossy enough, my body never thin enough and my house never that clean. Unless, like the adverts do, I Photoshop myself! Adverts are not real life. Real life is hair that goes frizzy sometimes and the occasional cat puke on the door mat, you tend not to see that in adverts.

Install ad blockers on computers and stop buying magazines to avoid adverts. Most women's' magazines are mainly adverts anyway and you can find articles about everything in the world online instead. Think about your most recent shopping trip, did you find yourself being drawn to things you had seen advertised recently? If you are sceptical try avoiding adverts for just a day or two and see if you feel less compelled to buy things.

Bargains are not bargains

Two for the price of one is only a bargain if you were going to buy one anyway AND you will be able to use 2 of them. Beware of getting sucked into the idea that a bargain is a good thing. Saving £50 on a £100 handbag that you were not intending to buy still means you have spent £50. Items in charity shops and sales are there because no one else wanted them, occasionally you might find a gem of a bargain but for me at least 90% of anything I have bought because it was reduced I have never used. If you want to spend money to fill up charity shops then bargain hunting is the way to go.

Have regular buy nothing days

If you walk past tempting shops daily go a different route. If you can go one day without bringing something back with you then you can do 2 in a row. You don't need to do this on your own: Buy Nothing Day is a global day of protest against mindless consumerism and is generally held in November. Instead of shopping people in over 60 countries around the world do fun things like shopping cart congas and zombie walks. For more information see www.buynothingday.co.uk and

www.adbusters.org/bnd.

Shop online for the boring things

Making a supermarket trip more interesting by spending money on things you do not need can be tempting. You can limit the risk of that by shopping for groceries online instead. That way you won't be anywhere near the book/ornament/kitchen gadgets that you might purchase as compensation for having to do something as mundane as grocery shopping.

Treat yourself with experiences and consumables

Rewards are good, it's nice to feel like you are treating yourself but this does not have to be with stuff. Spend money on meals out, cinema tickets, the theatre, massages or food and drink. There is research to suggest that spending money on experiences makes us happier than buying things. The reason behind this is that we get used to the things we buy, so that first flush of infatuation with a new pair of shoes is unlikely to bring the same level of happiness a couple of weeks later. We are more likely to talk about our experiences than our purchases and sharing what happens in our life can make us happier.[5]

Have rules

Give yourself some boundaries. If you have to go shopping take just enough cash for what you need. Stick to shopping lists. Leave your debit and credit cards at home. Do not look at eBay after a glass of wine. Just say no to new stuff.

One in, one out

By 'new' I mean new to you, this includes charity shop bargains as well as brand new things. If you get a new book, get rid of an old one you don't want any more. If you get a nice new jacket, evaluate any others in your wardrobe and get rid of the one you like the least. Think of this as upgrading your stuff. If you really do want to go out and spend some money, aim to get something that improves your life. Find something to replace another that wasn't working for you. Aim to take more things out of your house than you bring in.

---

[5] Gilovich, T., Kumar, A. & Jampol, L. (2015). A wonderful life: Experiential consumption and the pursuit of happiness. *Journal of Consumer Psychology, 25(1)*, 152–165. [click here to view paper]

Remember when you are shopping that you need to make room for the new thing in your home by getting rid of other things. Tip the balance in favour of less.

CHAPTER 9
Getting help from friends

Ask for help if you need it

Sometimes you really need to declutter quickly and there is no option to take it slow and steady. If you need to call in help from friends it is a good idea to set some boundaries before you start. Clutter is personal stuff and if the friend makes you feel judged and defensive when you go through it, that is not helpful. If you get an offer of help you only need to accept it if you want it.

Before you accept help, check the offer is genuine and that they are happy to do something mundane for you. Make it clear that this is not a free shopping trip for the helper. The stuff has to leave your home as soon as possible and it won't help if they hover over it like a vulture.

Explain that you are not asking them to decide if you want to keep things; you need practical help with no judgement or comments.

You can avoid problems when getting help with decluttering by choosing a helper who:

- has different interests to you
- is a different size to you
- has different tastes to you

Clarify expectations

Make it clear what help you need. No one else can make decisions about your things but they can provide practical help such as:

- Finding boxes to put clutter into
- Childcare
- Transport
- Sorting clutter into boxes for different destinations (charity shop, car boot sale, rubbish, etc.)
- Cleaning
- Providing moral support by listening
- Making tea and reminding you to take breaks
- Mending and DIY

Have a time limit

An hour's help with packing stuff or cleaning can make a huge difference. You are more likely to get things done in chunks than if you spend a whole 8 hours decluttering which would be exhausting.

Define the area you are decluttering

Have a goal in mind: do you want a cupboard sorted? A whole room?

Decide how you want it left at the end

Make sure you have time to clear up at the end and set an alarm so you can have time to put things back in place.

Moral support

Large decluttering sessions in short amounts of time can bring up all sorts of feelings about things. If there is no option to declutter in small doses and you have to go through this remember to be kind to yourself. If help is offered but you don't want anyone around when you sort through stuff you can always ask for moral support afterwards. Someone who will just listen to you by phone or in person can be as helpful as someone who drives all your clutter to a charity shop.

Chapter 10
Five guided days of gentle decluttering

5 Days of Easy Decluttering
Day 1 – Small stuff
Day 2 – Unfinished things
Day 3 – Kitchen drawer
Day 4 – "Just in case" stuff
Day 5 – Shelves or surfaces

The next five sections have detailed instructions for gentle decluttering. They cover different areas and types of clutter in your home. Each day has prompts and questions you can ask yourself to identify things you no longer need. Aim to declutter just 5 things a day to avoid getting carried away and stressed out. This nibbling away approach can make such a huge difference surprisingly quickly. Avoid decluttering anything that you are very emotionally attached to or that is valuable in the first week. Once you have decluttered stuff that is clearly useless you will be able to think more clearly about the trickier stuff.

Day 1
Declutter the small stuff first

Start small and deal with the niggly things first.

I have a house full of storage solutions collected over the years. I have wicker baskets, wooden boxes, ceramic pots and even nice cardboard boxes. They do work as storage but they also seem to attract the wrong things. My fruit bowl holds some apples and oranges, an expired voucher and a spare key. Some of those things do not need to be there!

If you tidy up by putting random things into containers, this strategy will help.

What sort of clutter ends up in bowls and boxes? If it is total rubbish it is easy to deal with. If it is more important, does it have its own place or is it in limbo?

Glance around your home and find the first bowl, box or container. Look into it, no need to tip it out, pick out 5 things that you don't need any more. If you can't find 5 things in the first container, move onto the next.

Checklist for small stuff. Ask yourself:

- Should it be there?
- Should it be thrown away?
- Is it part of something else long gone or broken?
- Do I like it?
- Do I need it?
- Do I want it?

The idea is to declutter in small easy chunks so you don't get overwhelmed and put it off.

If you find lots of things that should be in other rooms it might help you to have a new container for things that live elsewhere: one at the bottom of the stairs for things that live upstairs helps me.

Your goal for day 1 is to declutter 5 things, no more than that. It may seem like you will never get anywhere but this slow and steady strategy really does work. We all know that crash diets don't work and are not good for you. Decluttering too much at once can be soul destroying and it is easy to make mistakes. Remember it is fine to have stuff, just make sure it is stuff you enjoy having in your home.

DAY 2
Get rid of things you will never finish

We all start things with the best of intentions. Sometimes, we get distracted by other things and are left with lots of half done stuff. Having too many half finished projects around can put you under lots of pressure. It can make you feel like a bit of a failure, when in reality you have simply moved on to other things or become too busy.

Are there books you mean to finish? Can you even remember the plot? Some books are worth reselling on Amazon but you can usually find almost anything you want in a charity shop. If it's not been read, chances are it won't get read – ditch it.

How about half finished craft projects? If you genuinely think you may finish them one day then keep them. If not, why not give someone else the chance to enjoy them. I recently gave away a half-finished rag rug and I feel good knowing that it will actually get done now. Sometimes it's good to give someone else a chance at finishing the thing you started. There truly are some people who would be very happy to find a couple of square feet of unfinished patchwork in a car boot sale or charity shop.

Make room for something you can actually finish by getting rid of the things you know you won't.

Don't declutter anything that has a big resale value yet. Get rid of the things that are nagging you to finish them and making you feel bad for not having the time.

Some likely candidates are:

- Books and magazines
- Moisturiser that didn't quite suit you
- A bottle of liqueur too nasty to drink or cook with
- Craft projects
- Jigsaws
- To do lists
- Paintings and drawings

Checklist for unfinished stuff. Ask yourself:

- Do I like it?
- Would I use it if it was finished?
- What is its hassle factor to finish?

If you really are going to finish something stop reading this and finish it. Today, this moment, not tomorrow because that never comes.

At the end of day 2 you should have a box with 10 things in it. Ten things you are sure you do not want in your life any more. If you declutter 5 things a day, every week for a year, you can get rid of 1300 things easily!

Clutter control strategy for unfinished items

It is very tempting to start new projects when you get bored of a long ongoing one. If you are the sort of person who likes having lots of things to dip in and out of there is nothing wrong with that. If you find it is getting a bit out of control and nothing is getting finished, this will help.

Choose 3 projects each month

At the start of every month choose 3 projects to work on. One should be quick to finish, one should take the whole month and the other should be somewhere in the middle.

You can get the quick one out of the way if you like, then you can work on the other two when you have the time. If you finish one project, this will give you more time to work on the others. Do not add new projects until the start of the next month. At the very least, this method will help you to clear up some of those niggly things that only take half an hour to finish. At best, you will find yourself motoring through your tasks!

DAY 3
Declutter a kitchen drawer

Every couple of months I need to check my kitchen drawers for clutter. They are famously terrible places for clutter to gather and party. It is time for you to come down heavy on them and stop their fun.

Do you actually use the special tool that makes carrots into spirals? Does the toffee hammer see any action? If you use it, keep it. If you don't use it, will you ever?

GIve yourself 5 minutes to pick through the drawer. No need to turn it all out, just pick out what you don't need any more.

Checklist for decluttering kitchen drawer stuff. Ask yourself:

- Do I use it?
- Do I like it?
- Is it a part of something else I lost a long time ago?
- Does it need mending?
- Should it be there?
- If it's a tool, would a knife do just the same job?
- Have I got more than one of them?

- Do I need that many?
- Is it a nasty tangle of stuff that I am never going to disentangle?

If, on your way, you find broken things then throw them away or recycle them. You can count them in your 5 things per day too if you like.

The whole point of this is to get your home full of usable things that you like and that make you feel good.

If you don't fancy tackling a kitchen drawer try the bathroom, or your bedroom. Just 5 minutes for 5 things. It's easy. Choose small, not expensive, obvious things for today's declutter.

Mid-way through the week how do you feel? Is the donation box getting fuller? If you are having trouble making the days consecutive don't be harsh on yourself. Every time you declutter something you no longer need you are stepping in the right direction. If finding 5 things to declutter daily is too hard try dropping down to 3, or even 1.

DAY 4
Stuff that will 'come in handy one day'

Once upon a time I saw a brilliant project to make a dragon out of loo rolls. I cut it out of the magazine and put it 'somewhere safe'. By the time I had collected 4 carrier bags of loo rolls I had forgotten where I left the instructions. I kept the 4 filled carrier bags 'just in case' for about 6 months. I moved them out of the way many times, fell over them and replaced the carrier bags when they split. Until finally I realised it would never happen and I put them in the recycling box.

What are you saving it for?

Things we save for the future can be a varied bunch of clutter. Have you got:

- Chargers for phones long dead? – Sorry but they are probably obsolete now.
- Empty jam jars/bottles – Are you really going to make that jam? How long will it take you to replace your jar collection?
- Half empty pots of paint? – Top tip: decant into one of the empty jam jars and label with the room and paint colour. Then throw away the half empty pot.
- Ends of wallpaper rolls? – If you are keeping it for patching up walls how feasible is this? And how much do you need?

- Random bits of string/elastic bands/paper clips? – Can you find anything like this when you need it?
- Tins of beans for when all the shops close? – Eventually they rust, and are inedible.

It's easy to trick ourselves into thinking that we can save money by keeping things. It is far too easy to keep so many things 'just in case' that we can't actually find them when we want them. They take up space in our minds and in our homes.

If you are a storing type of person try storing with intent. For example, I keep a box of things that might be good presents for people so they are all in one place. This is very useful when you get a last minute invite to a birthday party. It is a good way to repurpose things you don't need yourself but someone else might love.

Checklist for decluttering 'handy' stuff. Ask yourself:

- Do I need it?
- Will I ever use it?
- Do I like it?
- Is it obsolete?
- Is it out of date?
- Is it still usable?
- Can I find it if I do need it?
- Is it cheap and easy to replace?

Your 5 things can go in your box, in the recycling or in the bin. You can count multiples singly or as a group depending on your mood.

Getting rid of 5 things a day is enough for this book so if you want to keep going be careful not to take on too much. It is possible to declutter in small daily manageable doses and get more done than in a total overhaul.

DAY 5
Decluttering shelves in 5 minutes

You can choose the things you keep around you. If everyone else around you thinks something is hideous, but if it means something to you, has good memories and makes you happy then keep it!

For everything else, here is a way to identify quickly what you don't need in your life.

Today, we are going to tackle one shelf or surface in your home. It can be in any room but as an easy start, choose the one nearest to you.

Checklist for decluttering shelves. Ask yourself:

- Do I use it?
- Do I like it?
- Is it a part of something else I lost a long time ago?
- Is it broken?
- Should it be there?
- Have I got more than one of them?
- Will I ever use it?
- Is it ugly?
- Is it something you mean to finish but probably won't?

- Is it something you are keeping because it was a gift but you don't like it?

If, on your way, you find broken things then throw them away or recycle them. You can count them in your 5 things too if you like.

The whole point of this is to get your home full of usable things that you like and that make you feel good. If your shelves are full of things that make you very happy then keep them. If they don't make you happy then why have them in your house?

5 minutes for 5 things. It's easy. Choose small, not expensive, obvious things for today's declutter.

If you have decluttered 5 things a day, by now you should have a box of things big enough to donate to a charity shop. Have you decided where to get rid of the box? Have you planned a reward for yourself when it's all gone?

If you haven't managed 5 things a day remember that even one thing a day is hundreds over the year. Start small and build up but there is no need to get rid of bin bags of your stuff every day.

BONUS
Control clutter in small containers

Those little pots and boxes seem like a great idea for keeping things tidy. Unless you have a system in place it is too easy for them to get out of hand.

This strategy will help you make your little containers into dedicated homes for things. You will then be able find them when you need them.

Grouping

What sort of things are in your small containers? Can you identify 5 groups that they would fit into?

Here are some ideas:

- Pens and pencils
- Hairclips and bands
- Keys
- Vouchers and tokens
- Spare change
- Mending things – buttons and safety pins
- Paper clips and pin tacks

- Cables, chargers, plugs and leads

Choose one group. Pens and pencils is a fantastic group to start with.

Find a box that will hold all the pens in your house and put it somewhere in the way. This is important because for the rest of the day you need to be looking out for pens and pencils and moving them into that box. If the box is in the way you will not forget about it.

If you have kids around this can be made into a game or a competition to soften the blow of tidying up!

Once all your pens are in one place you can check through them and decide if you really want to keep them all. Then, find one container for them so they have their own home. You might find it suits you to split this container and have more around the home in useful places too.

After you have conquered the pens, move onto the next item on the list.

Top Tip – you will be able to work out what groups of items you need by looking into the containers you have now. What is there a lot of? What do you use often?

Think about when and where you need things – do you do your hair in the bedroom, bathroom or hallway? That is where you need your hairclips. When do you empty your pockets or bags of spare change? Is it when you take your coat off? Could you have a spare change box by your coats?

When you have allocated places it doesn't matter if the bowls and boxes get intruded by things that shouldn't be there, because it will take you seconds to sort them out.

YOU CAN DO IT!

Don't just read about it

Try it out! Right now, wherever you are (unless you are in a supermarket because that will probably be frowned upon). Just look around you and see if there are 5 things that instantly stand out as total rubbish, not needed, liked or useful. If you have an empty box they can go into it, if you don't have a box find a carrier bag, if you don't have a carrier bag then put them in a pile near your front door so you remember to get rid of them.

"Lightbulb moment! You know that sinking feeling when you stagger off to bed ready to fall into it only to find it is covered in a pile of washing waiting to be put away? I was about to shift it from my bed to my chair knowing that I really ought to put it away, but the mere thought of doing so was exhausting. So I made a deal with myself, just 5 things, if I put away just 5 things I'll feel better about leaving the rest 'til morning (or whenever!).

Well there was a pile of 7 pairs of knickers so that seemed like a good easy place to start, but once the basket they go in was out I figured I might as well put the bra and pantiliners in too that go in the same one. I was about to put the basket back and figured that as it lives on top of the socks basket I may as well put those away too whilst it was so easy to get to.... and before I knew it I had the whole lot put away.

All because I figured I could cope with 'just 5 things' even though the whole pile felt far too hard." Anna

And if you find you like decluttering like this please come and join us in our very friendly and supportive Facebook Group at https://www.facebook.com/groups/lessstuff.

There are lots of resources, easy decluttering guides and walkthroughs at www.less-stuff.co.uk too.

Checklists

Are you ready to declutter?

- Do you have a decluttering box in an easy to get to place?
- Do you have a bin bag for rubbish and non recyclables?
- Do you know what can be recycled and where to take it if needed?
- Have you got a way of getting the unwanted stuff out of your house as soon as possible?
- Have you decided what you will tackle first?
- Have you planned a non cluttery reward?

Decluttering Checklist

Being clutter free does not mean having no belongings. This checklist can be applied to most decluttering situations and it will help you work out if you are keeping things for the right reasons.

Ask yourself:

Do I like it?

- Is it just plain ugly?
- Does it have a funny smell you can't get rid of?
- Do I like the colour?
- Does the texture feel nice?

Do I use it?

- Is it 2 sizes away from fitting me?
- Have I used it in the past 3 years?
- Have I opened it recently?

What is its hassle factor?

- Will I ever finish it?
- Does it need repairs I am never going to get round to?
- Will I use it if it is mended?
- Do I have the materials to fix it?
- Is it a nasty tangle of stuff that I am never going to disentangle?

Why am I keeping it?

- Am I just keeping it because someone gave it to me?
- Am I keeping it in the hope it will have value one day?
- Is it a part of something else I lost a long time ago?
- Would something else I have do the same job as it?
- Have I got more than one of them?
- Do I need that many?
- Is it cheap and easy to replace?

How does it make me feel?

- Does it have bad memories?
- Does it make me feel guilty?

If you love it; keep it, if you don't then ditch it!

Stop getting more stuff checklist

- Avoid adverts

THE ELEPHANTS IN THE ROOM

- Bargains are not bargains
- Have a buy nothing day
- Shop online for the boring things
- Treat yourself with experiences instead of things
- Have shopping rules
- If something comes in, something should go out

Re-cluttering checklist

Ask yourself the following questions when tempted by a new thing:

- Will I really use it?
- Does it fit me?
- Does it need fixing?
- Do I love it?
- Does it make me feel amazing?
- Do I only want it because it is a bargain?
- Have I already got one?
- How long did it take me to earn the money to pay for it?

About the author

Lisa Cole is an ethical designer who creates graphics and websites for small businesses and creatives at www.nakedwebsite.co.uk. She lives in Bristol with her teenage son and too many cats. Lisa was brought up with a make do and mend ethos and taught to hoard and save in case of disaster by her grandmother. The strategies in less-stuff are based on personal experience of dealing with having too much stuff. Lisa firmly believes that it is good for us to have things but that sometimes things take over and need dealing with. Lisa is not a minimalist!

Printed in Great Britain
by Amazon